# How to Buy a House and Walk Away a Winner

## Save Thousands of Dollars by Outsmarting Banks, Sellers, and Realtors®

Dawn Anderson

# Dedication

To the friends that are like family, and
to the half of my family that are like friends

For general information on other products or services, please contact us at 800-546-2289 within the United States.

**Published By** Midas Marketing and Media Group PO Box 27224, Anaheim, CA 92809

ISBN 978-0-6926-1871-4

# Table of Contents

# Chapter 1: Introduction

Buying a home is one of the largest investments you will ever make. If you are buying a first home, it is most likely the biggest investment you have ever considered. Closing escrow is a rewarding achievement. It is a relief when the quest for a home is over, and you have finally attained the American dream. But the process to get to that closing can be stressful, intimidating, and sometimes traumatic. I have seen marriages tested, and friendships and family relationships strained during the course of purchasing a home. Most of the anxiety comes from:

1- Not understanding what is affordable
2- Unfamiliarity with the loan process
3- Unexpected costs and curveballs

It is my goal to provide you with the information you need to make your home buying process simple and understandable. I have been a licensed Broker and Realtor® for over 15 years. During that time I have helped countless buyers and investors achieve their goals of purchasing a property. I am able to put to use my experience on behalf of my clients and share examples from past experiences in order to assist them in making the best home purchase possible.

That is exactly what I would like to do here. If you follow the recommendations provided in this book, you will be armed with the same knowledge and direction as my personal clients. The information contained in this book will help you avoid the hidden pitfalls and problems that confront many unsuspecting home buyers. You will face less intimidation since you will be more familiar with the terminology, jargon, and tactics often applied. You will recognize red flags as soon as they appear, and you will be equipped to act accordingly.

The goal is to get you in a home you love with the best terms, least amount of stress, and the greatest long-term potential.

In part, achieving these goals means you will be doing some of your own legwork and research. We are talking about entering into a financial obligation of thousands of dollars and in some areas of the country hundreds of thousands of dollars or more. Research needed for something of this magnitude is not the same as asking Uncle Bob's neighbor's nephew who happens to be a loan officer for advice.

By research, I mean gathering information to understand your credit profile, the home buying process, and the programs available to you. You will need to use that information to leverage yourself into a better long term position.

By being proactive and independent in your research, you will develop the knowledge necessary to make more informed decisions. You will also be less likely to settle for what is put before you because you will know that you have options.

So before hitting all of the open houses in your parent's neighborhood or browsing online at homes near your best friend, you need to have a clear understanding of the process, and your affordability.

Information is power, and once you know what lies ahead, you'll be able to handle it like a pro and walk away a winner.

.

# Chapter 2: Credit

Unless you are in a position to make a cash purchase, you will need to be familiar with your credit report and credit scores. You will need to know that there are three credit bureaus and five factors the bureaus consider to calculate a credit score.

## Credit Report

A credit report is compiled data of companies that have extended credit to you, the amount of open credit you have, and the amount of credit currently in use. The report also includes companies that have recently asked to view your credit, your current employer, and your current and past addresses.

The three U.S. credit reporting companies are - Experian, Trans Union, and Equifax. Each agency collects and records information about your credit and financial obligations that are provided to them. Information gathered includes your repayment history, status of current accounts, new credit inquiries, collections, number of paid accounts, and so forth. They can also contain information gathered from public records such as liens, judgments, bankruptcies, child support obligations, etc.

The FCRA was adapted to promote the accuracy of information in the files of the credit bureaus. The Federal Trade Commission (FTC), enforces the FCRA with respect to credit reporting companies. As part of the Fair Credit Reporting Act (FCRA) of 1970, everyone is entitled to one free credit report per year. This was put into place in order for consumers to review the accuracy of the information in their file.

If you haven't already requested your credit report this year, you may do so now by visiting the website annualcreditreport.com. The secure site is the official online site maintained by Central Source, LLC and sponsored by Equifax, Experian and Transunion as the centralized source to obtain all three reports.

If you do not have internet access, you may also call them at 877-322-8228 or submit a written request to

Central Source LLC.
PO Box 105281
Atlanta, GA 30348-5283.

When writing, include your full name- including a middle name or suffix if you have one, current address, phone number, and social security number. For your convenience, a link to a request form is included in the reference section in the back of the book. The annual reports are free, but they will not include your scores.

If you have already received a copy of your annual credit report earlier in the year, you can still request copies of credit reports direct from all three bureaus (at a cost), but these reports will not contain your credit scores either.

It is very important that you review a copy of your credit report from each bureau since mortgage lenders will be reviewing all three. This should be your first step in your journey to purchase a home, because you will want to have an opportunity to privately review the information contained in each report. You do not want wait until you are in the middle of a transaction to rely on a well-intentioned person telling you a bit of derogatory information won't matter a whole lot, when in fact that ding may prevent you from qualifying for the best terms available.

If you find any inaccuracies or outdated information, you may submit a dispute yourself and get the report corrected as I will explain later. A correction of an error can boost your score and mean the difference in rates or programs for which you qualify.

## Credit Score

A credit score is a number generated by each bureau for each person that has a credit file. The score is the result of an analysis of a person's creditworthiness, and each bureau has their own scoring formula. If you do not have a credit history, you will not have a credit score. Loan programs available to you as well as interest rates will be tied to your score and your credit report. If you do not have a score, you will not be able to get traditional financing.

There are five factors that determine credit scores: payment history, amounts owed, length of credit history, types of credit in use, and new credit. Since the formulas and the file information are different at each agency, you will most likely receive a different credit score from each as well.

The bureaus only evaluate credit and payment history that they have accumulated. A credit score does not consider income, and it does not consider loans or debts not reported to the bureaus -whether paid or unpaid. Also, sometimes credit information is provided to one or two bureaus and not all three. Since each bureau may receive different information, there may be a wide variance in the credit score number for the same person as a result.

Scores are updated monthly and will change according to the amount of credit used, length of time accounts have been opened, late payments, inquiries, and any derogatory information i.e.- collections, judgments, liens. It's very important before beginning your process that you know your credit score and review your credit reports so you can ensure all information is correct. Omitting potentially negative information that should not be on a report may raise your score. Higher scores usually mean qualifying for lower interest rates and higher loan values.

So how do you get a copy of your credit score? You have a couple of options. You may call a company with whom you have a current credit card to see if they provide that service. You may also request a credit score from the reporting agencies that create or distribute them, but you will have to pay for it.

Lastly, you may purchase a report and score online, or you can go to creditkarma.com and obtain your scores through them. CreditKarma.com currently does not charge for copies or reports or scores.

## No Credit

I have had some clients in the past tell me their credit is perfect because they have never borrowed a dime. While it is good not to have debt, it does not give a creditor an opportunity to evaluate your ability and willingness to pay on installment. So if you have no credit reported, you need to get some, or you may fall under the category of a "ghost." A ghost is a person who has never had a credit history or has had their history disappear over time. A ghost may be a college student, stay at home mom, someone who has lived overseas, or maybe a widow or widower.

Three open trade lines are usually preferred by lenders. If you have no credit cards or loan payments sometimes phone bills, utility bills or other obligations can be used by a lender to verify an "alternate account history." If you pay rent, you can also ask your landlord to report your rental payment history to the credit bureaus. Lastly, you may ask a friend or relative to add you as a joint holder of an existing credit account. You will be accepting joint liability for any charges, but this may also assist you in getting that additional credit line.

## Overuse

If you are using a lot of your available credit, it may be best to pay off some or all of your debt. Decreasing your debt will increase your scores and it can possibly increase your pre-approved loan amount. If you are using too much of your available credit, it may negatively impact your debt to income ratios (amount of debt vs. amount of provable household income) to the point where you may not qualify for a loan or the loan amount is less than what you want.

Credit cards with small limits and high balances may affect you more negatively than higher limit cards with balances higher than your low limit cards. For example, if you have a credit card with a $500. Limit and a $450 balance, that will have more of a negative impact than a card with a $5,000 limit and a $2,000 balance. To be safe, try to keep all cards with balances of 20-30 % of the limit or use one card for everything but emergencies.

Even if you think you may have too many credit cards, **do not close any accounts just before you intend to buy a home**. Closing an account may actually reduce your score for the short term, and you do not want to do that around the time you are in the process of buying a home. You may pay accounts down, but do not close them.

## Errors

As previously mentioned, if you find there is incorrect information on any of your reports, you may contact the credit bureaus directly to dispute inaccuracies. An inaccuracy can be an account reporting as open when it has already been paid, an account, judgment or lien appearing on your report that is not yours, or a late payment appearing when all payments have been made on time. There are other types of misinformation, but you get the picture. Look over the report and highlight anything that you believe is inaccurate.

Sometimes, especially in situations of very similar family names or Junior and Senior suffixes, it is possible to have information included in your report that is not even yours. Common last names often create confusion in reports as well, particularly frequent with judgments and liens. I remember an instance when a client with a very common first and last name financed a vehicle through a credit union. Another person with the same first and last name also financed a vehicle at the same credit union. The other person was late on her payments, but a Credit Union employee was reporting my client as being late- even though the social security numbers were vastly different, the vehicles were dissimilar, and the financing took place at different times.

Another example, a clerical employee from ABC retail transfers information to a bureau on an account that is 90 days past due. A couple of numbers on the social security number are transposed and the delinquency shows up on your account instead. Mistakes happen. So it is important to monitor your information to make sure there are no errors effecting your scores.

If you have late payments, collection accounts, or negative items on your report that are over seven years old, they have to come off of your account. It is the law. The time frame for the seven years begins as of the last time you made a payment toward the original debt. The exception may be bankruptcies and some judgments as they will stay on for up to ten years. If the original debtor has sold the account to a collection company, the clock does not reset (although some unscrupulous collection agencies may tell you it does).

Sometimes accounts are sold and resold again and again. Collection companies will still continue to try to collect. Old information should fall off automatically from your report, but sometimes it does not. That is why it is very important to review your report to make sure inaccurate and outdated information is removed. Cleaning up inaccuracies can improve your credit report, increase your credit score, and may be the difference between qualifying and not qualifying for a loan.

## Disputes

If you find incorrect information, you may initiate a dispute online or you may do so by mail. You may also begin with the creditor or collection agency, or you may go directly to the bureau. I suggest going direct to the bureaus. If you dispute online to one or more of the credit bureaus, the space to explain your dispute is limited. Selecting the mail option will allow you to submit as long of an explanation as you need as well as any documents to support your challenge.

If you select to communicate via mail, send everything certified mail so you will have a receipt for your records. Certified mail is a service available from the post office. It costs more than a postage stamp; however, the service provides you with a mailing receipt, a unique tracking number, and a record of delivery that the post office keeps for two years.

In addition to mailing the letter certified, you may also opt for a return receipt in which you receive a postcard back from the postal service showing the delivery date of the letter, and the signature of the individual who received it. This tracking information can also be supplied electronically.

The bureaus will allow you to submit an explanation and any proof you have supporting your claim. The Bureau will, in turn, contact the creditor and give them 30 days to respond to your dispute. A copy of a sample dispute letter is included in the Reference section at the back of this book along with contact information for the bureaus.

I recommend clients take an active part in disputing their reports rather than relying on a loan officer or paying a credit repair agency to do that for them. An agency may handle dozens or even hundreds of files at a time, and the outcome of your claim will not affect their ability to purchase a home. In other words, your dispute is not going to get the same personal attention as if you do it yourself.

Also, you do not want to get yourself in a position where you feel obligated to use a particular professional or company for a loan because of some assistance they provided. You never want to feel obligated to use a company. When you do, you put yourself in a position of dependence where you may not get the best deal. You want to be independent and choose the company that provides the best terms and service to you.

I can recall clearly one instance where a loan officer (not affiliated with me) actually quoted his client a higher interest rate than one that she actually qualified. He rationalized this because he noted a late payment recorded seven years prior to her applying for this loan. A late payment over 7 years old shouldn't even appear on the report any longer.

Rather than telling her she could get the information removed (or assisting her in obtaining the removal), he used the information as leverage to raise her qualifying interest rate. Why did he do this? Perhaps to make a higher commission, to meet his funding numbers, or some other reason benefitting himself. Because she was unaware of what was in her report and what she could do get it removed, she accepted the loan she was offered and lost money with a higher interest rate in the process.

You want to check your credit report and go over everything prior to contacting a loan officer so nothing like this happens to you. Catching a mistake before someone else does, realizing it can be corrected, and then getting it corrected can save you thousands of dollars over the course of a loan. No one is going to care more about the type of loan you obtain than you!

## Dispute Process

If you need to dispute information on your credit report or pay down cards or debt, it may take a month or two before the changes are reflected on your report. That is why it is very important to start this process prior to looking for a house. If you begin house hunting first, you may find a home with which you absolutely fall in love and cannot qualify to buy. The other scenario is that you may be able to qualify, but you end up getting a loan with less attractive terms than for what you could qualify. If the changes do not yet reflect on your report, you may be penalized with a higher interest rate or a loan program requiring a larger down payment. It may even reduce the amount for which you qualify or prevent you from purchasing the home altogether. Impatience can cost you thousands of dollars. It is best to make sure everything is accurate and then shop with authority.

Also, while you are in the process of purchasing a home, try not to do anything that will either have a negative effect on your scores or that may increase your monthly debts. Things that may have a negative impact would include excessive use of credit, opening up new accounts, making large credit purchases (cars, boats, furniture, vacations, etc.).

I have seen home buyers so excited about buying their new home run out to shop for and finance furniture only to be told later that their scores went down and they no longer qualified for the home loan. But you won't make that mistake because you are reading this.

Your credit report will be re-pulled and your employment verified just before your loan is funded. So no major purchases or changes.

So prior to speaking to a real estate agent or loan officer, you want to

1- Obtain a copy of your credit report and score
2- Review to ensure information is correct.
3- Make any corrections- pay down excessive debts, ensure 3 open trade lines, dispute inaccuracies

# Chapter 3: Mortgage Loans

There are many different types of loan programs suitable for many different types of borrowing needs. Prior to contacting a loan officer, it is important you have a basic understanding of the programs offered. You want to know at least a little about the programs so you have some control. You do not want to inadvertently end up with payments or terms in which you are not comfortable when you may be able to qualify for better.

I am not going to get into a great deal of loan analysis here, but I do want to include some information describing features of some of the programs available. This way, you will have a basic understanding and reference of what is out there before you speak to potential lenders. Once you understand this little bit about mortgages, it will be easier to speak with your loan officer. You will be able to ask great questions, and you won't accept anything blindly.

## Loan Categories

To begin with, there are basically two categories of mortgage loans- government insured loans and conventional loans. Government insured loans include FHA, VA, and USDA (RHS) loan types. They typically require a smaller down payment, and the credit requirements are usually lower than privately funded loans.

The other category of loans is the conventional loans. These are loans that are not insured, guaranteed, or backed by any government entity. About half of those loans are considered conforming loans. These loans require higher personal credit, lower debt to income ratios, and usually higher down payments.

The Federal National Mortgage Association (FNMA) also referred to as Fannie Mae does not originate or provide loans to borrowers. The government entity purchases mortgage securities, and they are restricted by law to purchasing single-family mortgages with origination balances below a specific amount. That specific amount is also known as the "conforming loan limit".

If your loan amount falls within the maximum loan limits of Fannie Mae, it is considered a conforming loan. If the loan exceeds the Fannie Mae limits, it is a jumbo loan. Since jumbo loans are higher dollar amounts, they carry a greater risk for the lender. As such, qualifying for these types of loans requires higher credit and the interest rates for jumbo financing are higher as well. Conventional jumbo loans are only restricted by the lenders themselves.

FHA and USDA Government loans will have a maximum loan amount, and that amount is based on geography (a link to websites identifying FHA maximum loan limits by area is included in the reference section in the back of the book).

VA loans do not have maximum loan amounts, but the VA loan guarantee program limits the maximum guaranty amount to the Fannie Mae conforming limit- which is currently $417,000.

New loan programs are constantly appearing in the private sector in order to remain competitive in the marketplace. Portfolio loans have unique guidelines created by individual lenders. These loans are not sold to investors, so these products may have features that other mortgages do not. For example, a portfolio lender might allow a borrower to use alternative forms of security for a mortgage for which he would not otherwise qualify.

# Government or Conventional

Your credit and the amount of money you have for a down payment may be the biggest factor in determining what type of loan you may want. As a general rule, if your credit score is in the range of 580-630 and the amount of money you have for down payment and closing costs is five percent or less, an FHA government insured loan may be best for you.

In terms of credit, if you have a score lower than 620, you would most likely need a government type of loan program to get financing unless you have a very large down payment. Lower down payment programs are more typical with government insured loans. FHA guidelines are more flexible about scores, discharge time for bankruptcies and foreclosures, and debt to income ratios.

If your debt to income ratio is low, and your credit history good, you may qualify for either option. What you will have to take into consideration then is the cost for mortgage insurance. If you do not make a down payment of 20% or more, your lender is going to require mortgage insurance. Whether the mortgage is government insured or privately insured, the mortgage insurance covers the lender in case of default. It does not cover the home buyer like homeowners insurance, and it is not tax deductible.

So with a down payment of 20% or less, your decision becomes do you prefer a larger down payment and a smaller amount of mortgage insurance each month or a smaller down payment of 3.5% for an FHA loan and pay more money in mortgage insurance each month?

If you have a Certificate of Eligibility   (COE) for a VA loan and the loan you want falls within the VA guaranty limits, this may be the first option you want to consider. The guidelines for VA loans offers a borrower to obtain a loan with zero down payment, although you will still have to pay a one-time funding fee. That amount varies according to the amount of down payment and the type of veteran, but the overall cost of getting into a home is lower than most programs requiring a down payment.

Also, if you have previously used your VA loan to purchase a home, you may be able to have your entitlement restored if the previously financed home was sold or the loan paid in full. Check with the Veterans Office directly to determine if there are additional requirements. Some loan officers are unaware that an entitlement may be restored, and they can incorrectly advise a borrower the entitlement may only be used once.

USDA loans are not talked about as much as other government loans. A USDA home loan from the USDA loan program, also known as the USDA Rural Development Guaranteed Housing Loan Program, is a mortgage loan offered to rural property owners by the United States Department of Agriculture. In order to qualify for a USDA loan, both the borrower and the property must qualify for financing. This program is for low to moderate income households, and properties must be located within a specific geography. Loan amounts may exceed 100% of the purchase price in some cases in order to address repair issues. You may look up properties by address on the US Department of Agriculture Rural Development website to see if they qualify.

## Loan Types

So now that you have an idea of the loan categories, you will need to know about loan types. By loan types, I am referring to the three most common types of loans, fixed rated, adjustable rate mortgage (ARM), and hybrids.

The most common and the most stable of the loan types is the fixed rate loan. The interest rate and the mortgage payment remain fixed for the duration of the loan term whether you select a 10, 15, 20, 30-year loan or something else. This option is usually best if you feel you're going to stay put and you will not be moving, upsizing, or downsizing in the next 3-7 years.

An ARM loan usually begins with a lower interest rate than a fixed rate loan but the interest rate is only fixed for a portion of the loan term. Some ARM loans adjust quickly after a couple of months but some ARMS are fixed for a number of years. These types of loan are called hybrid ARM loans. The adjustments on a loan are usually tied to some sort of financial index like the LIBOR, COFI, etc. There is no need to understand all of them, but you want to be able to look up the stability of a particular index in the event you decide to go this route. If you are considering an ARM, just be sure to ask your loan officer to what index the adjustment is tied. I will include links in the reference section so you may have a reference and look up that index to check the stability.

A hybrid loan may be beneficial if you intend to stay in the home for a short duration or if you intend to refinance within a couple of years. If that is the case, opt for a loan with a rate that is fixed for the time you intend to remain in the property like 3, 5, or 7 years. The interest rate will be lower than a fixed rate (saving you money), but the adjustment will not occur until the fixed has passed. You have to be careful with all types of adjustable rate loans because you never know what is going to happen to interest rates in the future. Incidentally, there are conventional and FHA ARM loans available.

By being familiar with some of the loan terms and loan types, you should feel more confident when searching for your mortgage loan, and better able to seek options that best suit your financing needs.

So prior to speaking to a real estate agent or loan officer, you want to

1- Calculate the amount of down payment
2- Determine if you want a government or conventional loan
3- Decide how long you will be in the property and review loan choices that align with your long-term plans

# Chapter 4: Getting Your Financing in Order

At this point, you know your credit score is as high as possible, and you are familiar with different loan types and categories. Now you are going to need a pre-approval letter before you start shopping.

The pre-approval is important at this stage for two reasons. First, it provides transparency of costs so that you may decide if you are truly comfortable with the numbers. I have seen cases where a person is pre-approved for a certain amount but when they discovered the corresponding payments, they felt they were in over their heads. Knowing ahead of time allowed them to adjust their loan amount downward. Secondly, a pre-approval letter will make your offer stronger. Since you have gone through the process of submitting documentation to a lender, you are also showing the seller and the agents you are not just a looky-loo. You mean business and you are ready, willing, and able to buy a home.

## Pre-Approval

Getting pre-approved for a loan is not the same as punching in a few numbers and pre-qualifying with a loan calculator on some website. To be pre-approved means that you have submitted income, financial, and other requested information to a lender. It also implies the lender has reviewed that information as well as your credit history.

Based upon the review, the lender will either request more documents from you or they will provide you with a letter stating you are pre-approved with them to purchase a home up to a certain price. The letter will also state the final approval is contingent upon other criteria that cannot be reviewed prior to identifying a home i.e. title report, appraisal, etc.

You need to go through the pre-approval process because it is important to have a clear understanding of 1- the loan amount for which you are approved 2- the costs associated with the home purchase and 3- the breakdown of your monthly mortgage payment.

Finally, you want to make sure at this stage the lender is confident in your file and with the program for which you qualify. There is nothing more heartbreaking than seeing a home buyer excitedly place an offer and they think they have a loan only to find out later they do not actually qualify. This typically only happens when a loan officer writes a quick letter as a favor and does not actually review income documentation, asset information, or perhaps even credit. The more information your loan officer gathers and you supply in the beginning, the better chances you will have of obtaining the loan expected with the terms discussed.

## <u>Choosing a Lender</u>

So how do you find a lender for your pre-approval? First let me e bit about the mortgage business. It is a "for profit" industry and people are going to make money off of your loan. That being said, you want to find a way to minimize the money being made off of you. That does not necessarily mean giving a call to your friend's brother who happens to be a loan officer. Nor does it mean relying solely on your agent for a referral.

Referrals and testimonials are important and should always be considered. But what I am saying is you should always use your own research and consider all of your options as well to ensure you are getting the best deal.

I have explained the difference between conventional loans and government loans. So what happens if you are referred to a loan officer who works for a company that does not offer VA loans or USDA loans? The person will most likely attempt to assist you within the scope of loan products offered by his company. In the case of a broker that only offers conventional financing, a person may not meet the guidelines of a conventional loan, but they may qualify for an FHA loan. The applicant may walk away thinking he cannot qualify for a mortgage, but maybe he just cannot qualify for the type of mortgage that brokerage has to offer.

Now that you are aware of the differences, you can make sure you can ask for specific products and not just settle for what one company is offering. If the broker or lender does not offer the type of loans you want, find another lender.

## Qualifying Process

The first thing your lender is going to do is request permission to obtain your credit report. They will most likely request a tri-merge report, a report containing information and scores from all three bureaus. Since you have already seen your reports and you have corrected any inaccurate information, there should be no surprises.

The loan officer will have you complete a Universal Residential Loan Application (URLA) commonly referred to as a 1003. This is a standardized form requesting initial information for each borrower that would be on the loan. Information such as name, current address, previous address, employment information, etc. The form also requests information on number of dependents, liabilities, assets and checkboxes for yes or no answers pertaining to declarations, etc.

In addition to the loan application, you will be asked to supply copies of documents that support the information you provided on the 1003. So you will be asked to supply pay stubs to support the income claimed, bank statements to verify assets, tax returns to verify income, and so forth. In the event you indicated in the declarations that you had a recent bankruptcy, you will also be asked to provide copies of the discharge papers as well.

If you have recently begun a new job in a different field or industry, you may want to wait a few months prior to submitting an application. Also, if there is an anticipated decrease (or increase) in work or income, you may want to delay as well.

Do not make any changes in the middle of your home purchase. In addition to supplying pay stubs and bank statements, all of your information will be reviewed again prior to the loan funding. So if you are in the middle of changing jobs, if you lose a job, or if there has been any change in your credit your ability to obtain financing may be jeopardized.

The lender will review the information you provided, and within three days of receiving it, they will send out a Loan Estimate. The Loan Estimate document replaces the old Good Faith Estimate and Truth in Lending disclosures. The form is easy to use, available in English and Spanish and is provided by law to avoid any misunderstandings of terms.

Since you have already addressed any credit issues, you should know the interest rate for which you qualify. Do not let a loan officer try to give you an interest rate for a credit rating less than yours. Speak up and if you do not get what you feel you deserve, move on to another lender.

## Debt Ratios

I briefly mentioned debt ratios earlier when speaking about types of loans. Debt to income ratio or DTI refers to total monthly obligations (debt) divided by total gross monthly income and multiplied by 100. There are two calculations with which a lender is concerned.

The front end ratio- also referred to as the housing ratio refers to the percentage of your income that would go toward your housing expenses, including the new monthly mortgage payment, mortgage insurance, real estate taxes, any HOA dues, dues.

If your proposed mortgage payment including taxes and any insurance is $1500 a month and gross monthly income is $6000, then your total front end ratio is 25 percent.

$$(\$1500/\$6000 \times 100 = \text{ is } 25\%)$$

The back end ratio indicates the portion of your income that is needed to cover all of your monthly debt obligations. This includes credit card bills, car loans, child support, student loans and any other debt that shows on your credit report that requires monthly payments. This also includes your new mortgage payment and other housing expenses.

If your proposed mortgage is $1500 a month for your mortgage and housing expenses, you have $500 a month in installment debts, your monthly debt payments are $2000. ($1500 + $500 = $2,000.) If your gross monthly income is $6000, then your total debt-to-income ratio is 33 percent.

**($2000/$6000 X 100= is 33%)**

Government loans will typically allow higher DTI's. Typically the lower the DTI and the higher the credit score, the better the loan terms.

You can control your DTI yourself by adding more income or decreasing installment debts. In that sense, you can also control the type of loan and the terms for which you qualify. Just calculate and address your DTI ratios prior to going through the pre-approval process. As with credit corrections, it may take 1-2 months before installment loan balances are updated with the credit bureaus.

## **Fees**

Fees are never set in stone. I have seen situations where loan officers have actually charged friends and family higher rates and higher fees. This happened because the home buyer did not know any better or because the loan officer knew his rates and fees would not be shopped because of the relationship.

A reduction in fees or an interest rate to you may also mean a reduction in that loan officer's commission, and that is why they are often set on not lowering them. This is not personal; it is just the business. And your loan officer is in business to make money too. I'm not an anti-loan officer by letting you know this. In fact, I owned a mortgage brokerage for years. I am merely stating the facts and cautioning you to shop – regardless of the relationship or referral source to the loan person.

A loan officer is typically paid a commission and that commission comes as a result either of the interest rate you are charged, the fees (loan origination, processing, etc.) you are charged, or a combination of both. It is usually the best decision to shop around to find out who is going to give you the best loan with the lowest fees.

When you do shop, you will probably run into at least one loan officer that tells you not to worry about the fees, because you can get the seller to pay for those. It is true you can absolutely ask the seller to pay your closing costs as part of the deal. But what happens when there are multiple offers submitted, both buyers offer the same dollar amount for the purchase price but only one buyer asks for closing costs?

The offer that nets the seller the most money is most likely going to be the one that gets accepted. I have seen home buyers lose out on their dream home because they ask the seller to pay the fees that their lender is charging them. This is not a good strategy for buying a home in a seller's market. So always look for the best combination of loan term, fees, and interest rate. Do not lose your dream home because of a lender's fees or a loan officer's potential commission check.

In order to obtain the best deal, let the loan officer know you are shopping and do not shop for more than a week or so. I tell you not to continue to shop because if you allow your credit to be run continuously, your scores may drop. If you have one or two inquiries within a one to two week period for the same purpose- mortgage inquiry, the scores should not be effected or the effect should be minimal.

If you have two lenders that are close and the difference comes down to fees, go to the loan officer with the higher fees and the same or lower rate. If you provide the lower estimate to that loan officer, he will usually beat it when presented with the paperwork. If he cannot, you will know that you have already negotiated the best deal, and go with the lowest estimate.

I mentioned looking for the best loan previously, and I did not mention the best rate. I did that for a reason. You do not make a "rate" every month, you make a "payment". You need to find the right loan product with the payment that is best for you. We have already touched on different loan categories and types - conventional loans, ARM (Adjustable Rate Mortgage) loans, Government Insured loans (FHA loans), etc.

Some of the loan types may have lower interest rates but they may also have mortgage insurance attached. So it's possible to have a loan type with a lower interest rate but a higher monthly payment than another type with a higher rate. Also, if you plan on staying in a property for many, many years, it may be best to avoid the attractive start rates of an ARM loan for the long term stability of a fixed rate loan.

A good loan officer will explain the loan types available so you can make an educated decision.

It is very important at this stage that you are comfortable with our loan officer and he or she is someone you feel you can count on and trust. You want to feel that this person is going to return your calls in a timely manner, provide answers to your questions, and work with all of the other players to complete the transaction on time with no surprises. If it is hard to get a return phone call in the beginning of a transaction, it may be harder to get one toward the end. So choose wisely.

## Know Your Limits

When going through the pre-approval process, the lender will take into consideration income from all borrowers, all debts and obligations that appear on credit reports or court documents (child support, etc.), and your credit profile.

If you have additional steady income other than traditional employment such as investment income, royalties, profit sharing, trust income, etc. You may also have that considered so long as you can show proof that it exists and it will continue to exist.

A lender reviews the debts and obligations that appear on a credit report. They do not take into consideration personal expenses like groceries, medical bills, gas money, utilities, entertainment, etc. As a responsible buyer, you need to look at the payment the lender is offering and add to all of your existing monthly expenses and the newly anticipated expenses. Along with your new house comes additional expenses- homeowners insurance, utilities, property taxes, maintenance, etc.

If you are comfortable with the house payment plus all of your other monthly expenses, it is full speed ahead and onto the next step. If the numbers do not seem like something you can comfortably handle, ask for a lesser loan amount. You do not want to end up being "house poor" where all of your money goes toward your mortgage and you have nothing left for anything else.

In choosing a lender, you want to-

1- Find the best loan and payments for your specific needs
2- Understand costs associated with loan
3- Decide on the loan limit with the payments most comfortable for you

# Chapter 5: Think about It

Buying a home is a BIG purchase. It is exciting and scary at the same time. You now have a letter from a lender that indicates they are willing to lend you the money you need in order to buy your dream home. Now, all you need is that home to buy. You need to figure out what you want, and then get in touch with a Realtor® that can help make that happen.

## Make Your Lists

Before you go out and look, make two lists. Make one list of the characteristics of your dream home. In other words, write down everything you want in your perfect home. Write down the number of bedrooms, bathrooms, lot size, and square footage. Is there a fireplace? Does the kitchen have gas or electric appliances? Is there a garage? How many cars will fit in the garage? Be as complete as you possibly can.

On the second list, write down what you absolutely need in your house. Can you get by without the family room? Will one and a half baths work for the time being? What if the counters are tile and not granite? This list of the basic needs should be much smaller.

It's important to realize before you start shopping the difference between what you need and what you want. I have seen home buyers that skip this exercise and place too much emphasis on the wants rather than the needs. That's the point where stress begins. The three car garage they want is $30,000 more than the approval amount so a call is placed to the loan officer to see if that loan can be increased to cover it. Or a buyer sees a completely remodeled house with all of the bells and whistles that just hit the market but there is no garage.

I have seen both scenarios. I have seen home buyers increase their buying power to above their comfort zone, and I have seen buyers kick themselves later for buying a home that did not meet all of their requirements because they were blinded by the "wow factor".

## Buy a Home to Sell

Many buyers cannot wait to buy a house near friends or family members or even close to their job. It is important to get what you want now. But it is also wise to purchase a home with the thought of selling someday in the back of your mind. You want to try to purchase a home in an area where values are likely to maintain so you can maximize your investment. As such, there are three criteria you want to research prior to buying the right home.

Schools- According to many, the quality of local schools may be the single most important factor when deciding upon where to buy a home. With that in mind, check out websites like greatschools.net district websites to see how the local schools are ranked and results of current test scores. Even if you are not a parent now, schools will affect the resale value.

Crime- Call up the local police department and speak to someone in the crime prevention unit. They will most likely be able to assist with statistics and such and provide some area guidance. There are currently two particular websites that are great for researching possible areas. Crimemapping.com allows a person to input an address and check out local crimes near the address and familywatchdog.us allows visitors to search areas for sex offenders.

Jobs and Economy- You want to know that the area has a stable and diverse employment.    The more people employed, the more stable the market.   If the area is lopsided in a single industry like high tech or auto, if that industry fails so will the local economy and probably housing.  If an area is diverse, the chances of stability are greater.

You will also want a property in fairly close proximately to shopping, entertainment, and transportation unless of course you are seeking something in a rural area.

In deciding what type of home is right for you, you want to consider-

1- Needs in a home
2- Area- schools, crime, economy, jobs
3- Buying a home that will sell

# Chapter 6: Time to Hire a Professional

At this point, credit is good, financing is in place, and you know the requirements of the home you want and the general neighborhood. It's time to hire your Realtor® and begin the search.

Many home buyers do not put in a lot of effort into finding an agent with whom to work, and that can be very costly. As a Buyer, you do not pay your agent a commission to assist you. Your agent is compensated from the gross commission offered by the seller. So would it not be smart to look for a Realtor® experienced in negotiating and who has sold many homes rather than settle on a referral to your sister's neighbor who just got a license or a friend of a friend who wants to sell part-time? You do not want to be a surgeon's first patient, and you do not want to be an agent's first client.

## What to look for in an Agent

The listing agent negotiates a commission agreement with the seller, whereby the seller agrees to pay a certain amount of gross commission upon the completion of the transaction. That commission is split between the listing broker and the selling broker. So you can shop around and retain an experienced agent who knows exactly the price a home should sell and will help you from overpaying, and it will not cost you a dime! The experienced agent can easily navigate you through disclosures, inspections, repair requests, and re-negotiations if necessary.

Your agent is like an attorney in that everything you tell that person remains confidential. As such, the seller cannot take advantage of the fact that you are pre-approved for $75,000 more than what you offered- because neither the seller nor his agent knows that fact. The privacy, advocacy, and the years of experience can be priceless… and the seller is paying for it!

There are two things you want to ask when searching for an agent. 1- Is the agent a Realtor®? All Realtors® are agents, but not all agents are Realtors®. Realtor® is a federally registered collective membership mark which identifies a real estate professional who is member of the National Association of Realtors® (NAR) and subscribes to its strict Code of Ethics. Realtors® are held to a higher standard.

An agent who is a Realtor® pays to belong to the Association. As members, Realtors® have greater resources at their disposal. Listings are inputted to the Multiple Listing System (MLS) within three days of being signed. Realtors® are all members of the local MLS. Not all agents are members. Did you know that some sellers and their agents only offer commission to MLS members only? If an agent does not belong to an MLS, they will not get paid by the seller if they bring a buyer to them. Do you think an agent that is not a Realtor® is going to show you all homes available or just the listings on which he or she will get paid?

The other thing you want to know is if the agent is going to show you all available homes on the market or just the listings from the agent office? Sounds like a trick question but some agents will cherry pick listings to show you. The selection is not based upon your criteria but on his! I have an independent brokerage, so I have never been caught up in the politics of real estate. However, some agents are **STRONGLY** encouraged to show and sell the listings of their own offices rather than other offices. Although to the public it does not make a whole lot of sense, many offices are more concerned about keeping their own sales statistics up and keeping commissions in house rather than keeping clients happy. Sad, but true.

Also, according to the NAR, nearly 40% of agents show houses based upon the amount of commission offered in the MLS. So if a commission on one house is 3% and commission on another house is 2% guess which house 40% of agents show their clients first? Sometimes this tactic can even create a situation where one property has multiple bids right away but a similar home in similar condition has no interested buyers. Look for an agent that shows everything!

2- Is the Agent an ABR® (Accredited Buyer's Representative) The Accredited Buyer's Representative (ABR®) designation is for real estate buyer agents who focus on working directly with buyer-clients at every stage of the home buying process.

If a Realtor® holds the designation of an ABR®, they have voluntarily taken and passed advanced courses in representing home buyers, and they been verified to have completed a minimum of 5 transactions in which they represented only a buyer in a transaction. So you definitely want someone who is a Realtor® and if they are an ABR® you have someone with verified experience.

## **Dual Agency**

A dual agent is an agent that represents both the buyer and the seller. It is not every day that you want to go out and buy a home, so you are not expected to know all the ins and outs and all of the details of such a major transaction. Some home buyers may think since an agent is already representing the seller they would have an edge if they have the same agent represent them as well. This can be a poor assumption.

When an agent represents both parties, your negotiation strategy can be weakened, and it could potentially be a costly scenario for everyone… but the agent. Don't fall into this agent trap. If an agent is representing a buyer and a seller, whose best interest is going to be served?

Say a buyer walks into an open house and really loves the property. The listing agent holding the open house sees how much the buyers like the property and advises them to put in an offer today before it is too late. The buyers are pre-approved for $250,000 but they want to offer $230,000. The agent now sees that the buyers are approved for a higher amount and goes back to his seller and informs him of that information. The Seller counters at $250,000, the buyers don't want to lose the property so they accept. By not using their own agent, they give up their negotiation strategy and in this case, it cost them $20,000. The sellers and the agent walk away the cash winners.

## **Be Protected**

As a home buyer, you want complete and fair representation in your real estate transaction? A real estate buyer's agent is responsible for protecting the best interests of his clients—buyers like you—and will guide you through every step of the process.

The two most important reasons to use your own agent is protection and efficiency. Most likely, the seller of whatever property you buy will be represented by a listing agent who will provide expertise throughout the transaction to the seller. Don't you want the same kind of service as a seller? A buyer's representative can provide you with the expertise you need through the entire transaction. According to research, buyers who work with a buyer's representative also find their homes quicker, while viewing more properties in their search, than buyers who do not engage a buyer's representative.

## Commitment

So how do you find an agent? There are several ways to search. If you want an agent that has an ABR® designation, you can go to the Real Estate Buyer Council website (REBAC) at http://rebac.net/buyers-rep and do a local search. You can also search online, or call a local realty office. You will want to speak to the agent a couple of times. The reason you want to do this is to see if they are going to return your call, follow up with you, or email you the information you may have requested. Sounds simple but one of the biggest complaints about agents is an inability to follow up. You want to make sure the agent is east to talk to, understands what you want, and follows up as expected. Once you have found this person, commit! Agree to work with him or her and make sure he or she agrees to represent you and help you find the right property.

I can't stress enough how important it is to commit to your agent, and have an agent that will commit to you. Until you find the right property, you will be working very closely together, calling and emailing often, and reviewing properties on paper and in person. Like any relationship, the more you are committed, the harder this person is going to work to please you and help you achieve your goals.

If you do commit and later discover the agent no longer returns calls or does not show you properties in which you are interested it is definitely within reason to seek another agent. You may do this so long as you have not signed an exclusive representation agreement. An exclusive representation agreement binds you to an agent for a specified amount of time. If you are asked to sign this written commitment make sure the agreement is for a short period of time-30 days or less. You can always renew after 30 days, but if you find out after a couple of weekends that you are not being shown everything on the market you have the option to find another agent after the 30 days. You don't want to be tied up with an agent not serving your needs for several months.

So in hiring an agent you want to-

1- Find an experienced Realtor® who you feel comfortable with and who will work for you as a Buyer's Representative to protect your interests
2- Avoid dual agency
3- Commit when you find an agent

# Chapter 7: Types of Home Sales

Most home sales referred to previously are standard, fair market transactions.  The house has been lived in, and the conditions of the property vary.  But there are several other types of home sales that you may come across.

## New Home Sales

New homes are purchased direct from the builders.  Typically there are several highly upgraded model homes that you may walk through to get an idea of floor plans and options.  Many times, you will be dealing direct with the builder's sales agent who can assist in writing up your paperwork and helping you pick out your options and upgrades.  I have seen standard houses with start prices in the $200,000's and by the time the "optional upgrades" are added, the price comes out well into the $300,000's. Stunned home buyers can easily end up way over budget, and they do not realize it until closing time.

Most home buyers do not have an agent with them when looking at new homes, but before you visit on your own, there's one thing you need to do.  Prior to visiting the models, call the office and ask if they offer a broker co-op.  You are essentially asking them if they would pay your broker a commission.  Depending on the market, most builders offer 2-3% broker co-op for the courtesy of an agent introducing their clients to them.  So if the builder offers a co-op, ask them if you do not bring an agent if they will agree to reduce the price by the same dollar amount they quoted for the co-op.  If they will not reduce the price, bring an agent. After all, you will not be paying the agent commission, and the commission will not have an effect on your price.

An agent can in some instances provide protection to you against unusual fees or charges that may appear. If you are financing, the builder may offer you "incentives" if you will use their affiliated lender. Prior to agreeing, remember to shop. I have seen several instances where the builder incentives were not close to covering the cost of the higher loan costs of the internal lender.

The sales staff in the office of the home builder are licensed real estate agents, but they are also sales people already representing the seller (remember dual agency). They have to get the lots and homes sold, and they are there to sell on behalf of the builder. Having your own agent may help facilitate the transaction and get rid of some of the charges that buyers often fall prey.

## Short Sales

When a homeowner owes more on the property than the current value, the transaction is considered a short sale. A short sale involves several steps not applicable in traditional sales. Since the current lienholder has to write off a large amount of current loan in order for the sale to transpire, the lender(s) involved have to approve all pricing, terms, etc.

If you are browsing listings and you see a property advertised significantly less than nearby properties, the chances are very good that it may be a short sale. Agents will very often drop the price to a very attractive amount in order to receive quick offers perhaps to stop a foreclosure sale. Since the low price has not been approved by the lender, buyers are lulled into thinking they may have found a great bargain. This usually is not the case.

The lender will send out either an appraiser or local broker to value their asset, and they will sell the property at fair market value. The price may be slightly discounted because it will be sold as is, and without any repairs. Although the buyer may have an inspection performed, the lender who is now acting as the seller, usually will not pay for any repairs – including termite damage. So while the property may be purchased at a slight discount, the buyer will be increasing their risks well.

Some buyers look blindly at the sales price and by the time repairs are factored into the cost, they end up paying more for the property than current value. If it looks like a great bargain on the outset, you really need to look at the numbers. If you find a home $20,000 below neighborhood sales but it requires $40,000 in immediate repairs, it is not a bargain. In fact, you may end up overpaying.

## Foreclosures

Like short sales, foreclosed properties are typically sold as is. One of the draw backs of a foreclosure for inexperienced home buyers is that there is no one to ask or to provide disclosures about the property or its history. So whereas an owner occupied house has someone to tell you if there have been electrical issues, a death on the property or problems with neighbors, a foreclosed property has no one to tell you the history.

In the case of foreclosures, home inspections become even more important. The inspector may find areas of question, but since you will be unable to ask the previous owner any questions, you will be even more reliant upon his expertise and recommendations.

You can do some investigating by speaking with neighbors and you can ask your agent to order a CLUE (Comprehensive Loss Underwriting Exchange) report. The CLUE report will provide an insight into any recent insurance claims against the property. You would be surprised at the willingness of most neighbors to let a prospective buyer know about the previous owners and if they are aware of any major repairs or issues. It is very important to take a proactive role of inspecting when buying a foreclosure.

## **Probate**

Lastly we have probate sales. Probate sales are a legal process in which a court oversees the settlement of an individual's estate after his death. The person representing the trust may or may not have had any knowledge about the condition of the property. As such, many disclosure items typical in a standard sale are exempt within a probate sale.

The sales require a different purchase agreement form than a standard sale, and the price and terms may or may not need court confirmation. Probate sales may require a larger down payment than typical sales depending on court guidelines. In the event court confirmation is required, the terms may be subject to overbid. That means even though you have a signed purchase agreement for the purchase, someone else may overbid in court and they could purchase the property. You can also bid against others to retain the rights to purchase.

I have seen cases where a buyer thought they were getting a really great deal on the property only to have several bidders show up in court only to outbid him. So if court confirmation is required, your purchase price may change.

So when looking for a home you need to

1- Understand the type of sale
2- In a short sale or probate sale find out if the price has been approved
3- Ask your agent if he/she is experienced in handling the specific type of sale

# Chapter 8: Start Looking

After you have aligned yourself with an experienced agent ready to sift through homes negotiate on your behalf, it is time to team up and begin the journey. I say journey, but I have had instances where the first house I showed a client turned out to be the dream home.

## **The Process**

In the most effective searches, your agent is working on your behalf and you have been supplied with a website where you can look at updated listings along with listings your agent sends you. The Internet is a blessing in that buyers are now able to view and tour properties online 24 hours a day, and scope out the geography by using Google Maps and Google Earth. It is now possible to do this with homes around the corner and across the country. So it is time to hand over your needs and want lists to your agent, and begin working.

At this point, less experienced buyers may start racing in and out of open houses, and unleash friends and family to assist in the home search. I cannot stress enough the importance of remaining calm and sticking to the budget and needs list. Remember the example... using the Seller's agent cost the buyer $20,000? You do not want that to happen to you.

The more people that become involved in the search, the more the search becomes stressful. I have had clients with strict budgets who received constant pressing from friends to look at more expensive homes because "the seller may take less." I have seen clients fall in love with house after house above their budget only to have their low offers rejected or countered to a number that they could not afford. Rejection leads to frustration and stress. You don't want that.

Work closely with your agent who will communicate with other agents, search information that the public is not privy, and identify potential properties for you. Your agent should be in contact with you daily- if not a couple of times a day to review properties and schedule showings for times convenient for you. I tell my clients it may only take seeing one home or it make take seeing hundreds. But when you walk into the right one, you will just know.

## Neighborhood

Once you find a home that you are considering, it is important you do some due diligence on the neighborhood. I have already mentioned location as something to consider when shopping. You should already be aware if it is near shopping, schools, etc. Now that you have found a potential property, you need to check out the neighborhood at different times of the day.

Take a look around and notice the types of vehicles parked in the driveways and on the streets. Take notice if the lawns and exteriors are well maintained or if there are any signs of graffiti. Sometimes bars on windows are a sign of ornate decoration; but sometimes, they can be a sign of concern.

If it is important to have children in the neighborhood, take a drive around the area when school gets out to see the amount of kids. Drive by in the evening to see the amount of traffic and to see what the noise is the area is like.

If the property is near train tracks or a busy highway, sit in your car with the windows open to see if it's something that would be a factor. Although double paned windows may shield you from the noise when you're on the inside of the house, you may want to get an idea of the noise if you are going to be in your backyard.

You can always remodel the interior, and you can even add onto the structure. You cannot change the neighborhood.

## Concessions

Remember the two lists you wrote out? Here's where they become important. When you start to look at houses, you have your list of needs. A good Realtor® will show you only homes that fit your "needs list." If you need a garage, all of the homes shown or sent to you should have garages; if you need a single story, all of the homes should be single story, etc. From the group of homes that fit your needs, you take out your list of "wants" and everything you look at should be a variation of prices within your range and amenities from your wants list.

## Buyer's Market vs. Seller's Market

Pricing is going to be dependent upon the current economy and whether you are dealing with a buyer's market or a seller's market.

A buyer's market is when there is an abundance of inventory and buyers are able to keep prices down. It is reasonable that a day or two to make a decision will not have much of an effect since properties tend to sit on the market. During this type of market, it is more likely that a Seller may agree to pay some of the buyer's closing costs or agree to a reduced price. This, of course, depends upon how motivated the Seller is to move.

Offering a reduced price will depend on whether there have been price reductions to a point that the current list is below market already. But since there is a scarcity of buyers, there's a good chance of paying less than the original list price.

A seller's market is when there is a shortage of inventory and sellers are able to keep prices high (so buyers have to be smart and prepared if they want to get the right house at the right price).

In a seller's market, desirable listings may be sold in days or even hours. This means there is a shortage of inventory and an abundance of buyers. It is probably a good idea to offer list price or maybe even above list so long as the comps can support the price.

There are some things you can do in a seller's market in order to make your offer stand out. First, you can offer a quicker than usual close. Speak to your loan officer first, but if he can pull this off it can really be attractive to motivated sellers. Even if they are not in a position to close in say 20 days, by showing them you are indicates you are a strong buyer with paperwork in order.

Secondly, you can increase your earnest money deposit. Putting more money at risk also shows the sellers you are serious. I had a situation back when homes were selling within hours. I had clients who looked at house after house and we were coming up short. Finally, we found a home that just came on the market, and there were already offers. As a Hail Mary, they put down a fifteen percent EMD, which amounted to $60,000. The sellers knew we were serious, and we got the house.

As a last resort, you can always offer an amount much higher than the list value. You can do this with a financed offer or an offer contingent upon an appraisal. In the event the appraisal comes in lower than the offer amount, you can try to renegotiate. Since you're already in an escrow, sellers are more apt to negotiate with you. The only problem with this tactic is that a seller can counter your terms and ask for no appraisal contingency. At this point, it might be best to walk away if you know the price is too high.

If sales don't really reflect a buyer's market or a seller's market, there is such thing as a balanced market. This is when supply and demand of homes are in line with one another. In this type of market, an offer should be made in a reasonable time and it is usually standard to ask for some closing cost assistance or offer a price less than list. Again, offer a reduced price if the comps support it, as most sellers expect a lower initial offer leading to some negotiating.

Because you have already gone through the pre-approval process, you will be prepared for any type of market and that will put you ahead of many other buyers.

If financing does not apply to you and you have all cash, you are one of the most sought after buyers. You may close quickly and without contingencies. Your funding will not be delayed and you have no lender working at a snail's pace holding up a transaction.

Because of the low maintenance nature of cash buyers and because the likelihood to close on time without issues is much greater than a financed buyer, they are often selected over financed buyers. Many times, they are selected even when their offer may be lower.

To a pre-qualified buyer, this may seem unfair. But a cash buyer is many times preferred because there will be no further negotiations if appraisals don't come in at value and there are usually no delays. But as a cash buyer, do not think that a seller is going to lose too big of a chunk of money to accept your offer.

I have had cash buyers offer five to ten percent below listing price even in a seller's market because they overvalued their position. A cash buyer can many times offer less; however, when you begin offering $10,000-$20,000 plus- less than list price, you have to put yourself into the shoes of the seller. If the seller is patient for a 30 day close with a financed buyer and no appraisal issues, he will have made $10,000-$20,000+ in a mere two to three weeks just for being patient.

As a cash buyer, your offer is preferred as long as it's reasonable.

## **Stick to Your Budget**

When looking for a home- especially in a Seller's market, it can be very stressful when the right home just isn't coming up.

First, do not look at anything above your budget. I say this from experience. Clients will walk into an open house or just happen to see a home in the right area. After seeing it and falling in love, they find out the home is over their budget. They inevitably begin to compare every new home they see to that more expensive home.

This can be very frustrating. Some clients will even go so far as to try to be pre-approved for a higher loan amount (outside of their comfort zone) in order to obtain the more expensive property.

If you have already decided on a strict budget, do not go above your comfort zone. It is easy to rationalize that you can cut a few expenses here and there to afford it. Again, you do not want to be house poor.

I remember representing a couple and showing them house after house within their budget and within their criteria. They were not finding anything they really liked. They eventually switched agents. Their new agent showed them a beautiful modern a condo with a price tag $30,000 higher than what they originally budgeted. It was smaller than the properties I was showing, with a one car garage rather than a two car garage. The agent referred them to a loan officer friend, and he was able to qualify them for a higher loan amount. The new loan was an ARM loan and a stated income program. The couple purchased the home and in less than one year, it was listed in the MLS again as a foreclosure. They fell in love with the "wow factor," and ignored their budget. They bought the home, but they also ended up losing the home in less than one year. Do not ignore your budget.

## Writing the Offer

Once you find the home within your budget and meeting your requirements, your agent will provide you with neighborhood pricing information in the form of a Comparative Market Analysis (CMA or comps). This information is important because it will tell you the price at which what other similar properties are selling and at which they have sold. You want to make sure the price you offer is in line with the property. You don't want to offer too much or too little, and the data provided by your agent will help you. You did your research in selecting an experienced Realtor® so consult with your agent and take advantage of the experience.

It is very important to understand the seller is never obligated to send a counter offer. I remember one anxious first time home buyer who insisted on offering less than asking price upon the advice of her friend. The friend had it all figured out. The seller would counter, and they would eventually agree on a price in the middle of list price and original offer. In this particular case, the seller accepted an offer higher than list, and the buyer was left broken hearted because she lost a property she truly loved. Incidentally, this was done in a seller's market.

So make a serious offer when you find a house you love, and know that the house will still have to appraise. You will have an opportunity to inspect the property completely. If the list price is way above reality, do not be afraid to offer what you believe is fair market. Have your agent write a note with supporting information (comparable sales) to explain why your offer is low. Some sellers just price high and they need to hear the facts. A realistic seller will take the facts into consideration and either counter or accept your fair market offer amount.

It never hurts to let the sellers know a little about you. I would suggest writing a brief letter about you and your family. If you have kids, let the sellers know how much they look forward to growing up in the house and neighborhood. If you do not have kids but plan to grow your family in the future, tell them you were waiting to find the perfect house before having children and this is it.

Let them know about your career, and why you want to live in this particular neighborhood. Personalize your offer and let the sellers know you appreciate what they have done to the property. Ensure them the home will be going to someone who will continue to care for the property. You do not know how many other offers will be submitted along with yours. This may sound cheesy, but you want to do everything you can to get an edge. I have seen sellers take lower priced offers simply because they like the buyers.

So in looking for a home you want to-

1- Provide your agent with your needs list
2- Make you offer based on fair market value
3- Personalize your offer and let the seller know about you

# Chapter 9: Breaking Down the Offer

Since you will be most likely using the services of a Realtor®, your offer will be written up on a standardized form. The forms are specific according to the state and local associations. All forms will include certain pertinent information- date, offer amount, deposit amount, down payment, financing, escrow period, inspection time, and allocation of costs of certain items. Other information included in the offer such as liquidated damages, key transfer, addendums included, etc., may vary according to local disclosure laws.

It is very important that prior to signing the Purchase Agreement you have a clear understanding of the terms and your responsibilities as a party to the agreement.

## <u>Deposit</u>

The Purchase Agreement would have specified an amount for a Good Faith Deposit or Ernest Money Deposit (EMD). In California, the deposit is money is placed into an escrow account by a buyer to show that he or she has the intention of completing the deal. This money is typically required to be deposited upon the buyer's acknowledgement of the seller's acceptance or within 3 days.

Once the money is delivered to escrow, instructions will be generated, and the transaction opened.

If the deposit money is not delivered in the time frame agreed, the transaction may be cancelled. Also, if during the inspection period the Buyer discovers information about the property, area, or condition that causes concern, the transaction may be cancelled and the Deposit returned to the buyer without penalty.

If the Buyer fails to perform or cancels without cause after timeframes have passed, the deposit may be at risk.

## Down payment

The down payment refers to an initial payment made when purchasing a home on credit. The lender will verify this amount has been deposited to the settlement company, and the settlement company will ensure this amount has been collected prior to recording.

Since you have already been pre-approved, the down payment amount will have already been determined and discussed with your lender. The amount of the down payment and the financing terms may be reviewed by the seller as the type of loan and financing you are using to make the purchase. The higher the down payment, the stronger the offer. This information will match up with your pre-approval letter.

## Time Frames

Times frames in a purchase transaction are very important for both parties to adhere. The offer is valid for a specific time frame, the buyer has a time frame to deposit the earnest money, the escrow shall last for a specific time period, and the seller must turn over the keys by a certain date. Likewise, documents must be delivered within certain windows, contingencies removed, and inspections completed. The time frames are specific in order to ensure the transaction moves along and to make sure everyone is aware that the transaction may be in jeopardy if the guidelines are not met.

There may or may not be counter offers involved. As previously mentioned, the seller is not obligated to counter any offer nor are they required to select the highest offer if there are multiple offers. In a seller's market, write an aggressive offer at or above list price. In a buyer's market, write an offer within the range of comparable sales and you may want to ask for some closing cost assistance.

Once the purchase agreement is fully executed- signed by buyer and seller and buyer has acknowledged seller's acceptance, the agreement will be sent to the settlement agent who will facilitate the closing of the transaction.

## Allocation of Costs

There are costs associated with a home purchase in addition to those associated with your lender. There will be settlement fees (escrow fees), title fees, Natural Hazard Disclosure fees (NHD), notary fees, wire fees, etc. If the property is located in a homeowners association (HOA), there are also HOA doc fees, HOA transfer fees, and in some cases private transfer fees. It's important that the responsible party for each fee is specified in the agreement to avoid confusion later.

Typically (but not always) escrow/settlement fees are split 50/50. That means buyer pays for their own escrow fees and a seller pays for theirs. In California, it is typical for a seller or seller's agent to select the escrow company. While that should not be an issue in most cases, some escrow companies are affiliated with the seller's brokerage. As such, you will want to verify that as a buyer, your escrow fee is the same as the seller's. It is unfair for an escrow company to provide a discount to a seller because of an affiliation and not a buyer. I am not saying this happens a lot, but I am suggesting you verify the fees. It makes no sense paying more for escrow than a seller.

The Seller typically pays for an owner's title insurance policy, and the buyer will pay for a title insurance policy covering their own lender. Sellers also typically pay for transfer taxes and from county, city, HOA, or private transfers. HOA associated fees, NHD fees (if required), are usually agreed to be paid by the seller.

A buyer is strongly suggested to obtain a home warranty plan either purchased by the seller or by themselves. A standard home warranty will cover the repair or replacement of major appliances for up to a year after the close of escrow. There are optional coverages available like extended roof, plumbing or pool equipment coverage. Links to some larger home warranty companies are included in the reference section.

When writing up your offer, it is important to double check-

1- The amount of the deposit that you will need to provide upon acceptance
2- The down payment and financing disclosed to the seller
3- The time specified time frames so you may act accordingly

# Chapter 10: 30 Days from Home

Once your offer is accepted, you will receive a flood of paperwork from agents, escrow, and your lender. It's best to stay organized and stay calm. All of the professionals involved have probably successfully completed hundreds of transactions between them. If you have any questions, never be afraid to ask.

## Disclosures

When each party uses a Realtor, you can usually be assured that there will be more disclosures and more paperwork. This is a great thing as you will have more information on which to base your purchase decision as opposed to a FSBO (for sale by owner) transaction where the owner may not know that they need to disclose a leaky roof or active plumbing issues to a buyer.

The amount of disclosures will vary by state and even county. Currently, a buyer in a Southern California standard transaction may expect to receive about 30 pages of CAR (California Association of Realtors) forms plus a Natural Hazards Report of an additional 45 pages or more. The disclosures help facilitate communication and transparency between both parties so the Buyer is fully aware of the condition of the property to be purchased.

In addition, the Purchase Agreement allows for an inspection period. During this time, the Buyer is able to hire a professional inspector to physically inspect all aspects of the home. In some cases where a question might arise, the inspector may suggest an expert such as a licensed electrician or a roofing contractor be consulted as well. The Buyer is able to bring in and have professionals and experts inspect the property so that all questions of condition are satisfied.

The seller is expected to disclose all material facts concerning the property, and the buyer is expected to do their own due diligence as well. The key to all of the disclosures is the have buyer fully aware of any condition(s) the Seller may be aware of.

## Home Inspection

All home buyers are recommended to have the home inspected prior to purchase, so please do it. An inspection by a professional may cost a couple of hundred dollars, but it could save you thousands by either uncovering matters that can be negotiated and addressed or by uncovering issues that prevent you from wanting to continue with the purchase.

I typically do not recommend a particular inspector or company to my clients; but I do recommend they find a professional with experience, errors and omissions and liability insurance. As with Realtors® and most other professionals, insurance coverage is important in the event of an unforeseen issue. I have seen out of work contractors represent themselves as home inspectors, and I have heard of instances where home buyers have had friends or relatives act as inspectors to save the couple of hundred dollars it costs to hire a professional. Home Buyers have a responsibility to inspect the property just as a seller has a responsibility to disclose. It is best to use the services of a person or company who is willing and able to take responsibility in the rare event of an oversight or mistake. I will include a links in the back of the book for home inspector information.

A home inspection is a comprehensive physical inspection of a property. The assessment includes roof, exterior of the property, electrical systems, plumbing, attics and crawl spaces, heating and AC, windows, doors, etc. In the event there is a pool or spa, those items may be inspected for an additional charge- depending upon the inspection company. Also, if there is a concern of mold or other issues, the inspector may perform tests for additional fees, or he may refer you to other professionals.

Depending on the age of the home, there may be a very long list of repairs. Remember, you are paying a professional to inspect everything, so he is going to be as complete as possible –from scratches on floor tile to missing junction boxes in the attic. You will be provided with a written report so you can reference and share with the seller if there are safety items that need repair.

Home Inspectors do not make repairs themselves as that would be a conflict of interest. If the inspector notes an area of damage or concern, that will be included in a report- usually with photos to support the finding.

If your inspector finds items in need of repair, you and your agent will need to discuss your options. You can request items to be repaired, request compensation or price reduction in lieu of repairs, or in severe cases you may cancel the transaction. Typically, sellers are most apt to negotiate repairs that are considered safety issues and may not be amenable to cosmetic issues. You are buying a used property so expect to have some issues and wear and tear unless it is new construction. If the repairs are not major, try getting a price reduction or credit. It will feel like an extra added bonus.

Any repairs agreed to be completed by the seller will be completed prior to the close of escrow.   Prior to the close and before you sign the loan documents, your agent will schedule a final walkthrough so you can verify the repairs have been made and so you can see that there have been no other changes or alterations and the property is in the same condition as you expected.

In most cases, one of the agents will have requested a termite company inspect the property and generate a report of findings. When financing a property, a lender is going to request a termite clearance certificate. The reports are usually divided into two sections.   Section 1 includes a list of existing damage- evidence of termites, dry rot, etc.   Unless a property is being sold as is, the Seller will usually handle all of the Section 1 items at the Buyer's request. Section two repairs are those that are preventative in nature and if left unattended may become an issue in the future.

It is not uncommon for section 2 to be blank.  If there are section 2 items, depending on the nature the lender may not require them to be addressed prior to close.  In the event there is an issue, payment would have to be negotiated as well as who is to pay.

So what happens if the inspector uncovers major issues?   If the issues are major and they have not been disclosed, you will have to decide whether the home is worth the risk.   If there are problems beyond the scope of normal wear and tear like major plumbing, roofing, or electrical you would be well advised to have the seller pay for the complete repairs.  If there is a significant mold issue or foundation problem, it may be best just to walk away.

Even If the Seller agrees to reduce the price, that will have a minor effect on your monthly payment and down payment.  You will still have to come out of pocket after close in order to make the repairs.

Also, once you begin repairs, you don't know if other issues will be uncovered. Do not fall in love with a property so much that you overlook costly repair items.

## Lender Paperwork

Concurrent with the review and signing of the disclosures and escrow paperwork, and the home inspection, your lender will be in close contact as they will have additional paperwork for you as well.

Now that a property has been identified, your loan officer (if he hasn't already) will be gathering updated paperwork for you in order to submit to underwriting. By updated paperwork, I am referring to most recent pay stubs and bank statements. All other documents tax returns, divorce decree (if applicable), retirement accounts, etc. should already be in the file.

It is at this point where you definitely want to review the paperwork and disclosures the lender sends to you and make sure the rate, fees, and loan terms are all that you expected. Since you shopped for a good loan officer, there should not be any ambiguity at this point. If there is, you will need to clarification immediately and before proceeding any further.

I have seen instances where loan officers did not thoroughly review a buyer's paperwork prior to the pre-approval and all of a sudden the buyer doesn't qualify for the same program once the escrow has begun.

This is why before even shopping for a home, it is imperative to have good communication with your loan officer and a definite understanding of your approval. It is possible and even common that interest rates may fluctuate slightly as a result of the market.

After an escrow is opened your loan officer should not give you a call stating you now need a down payment of twenty percent when he previously pre-approved you for a five percent down loan.

## Appraisal

As soon as possible, the lender will order an appraisal of the property. An appraisal is an estimate of the property's current value taking into consideration factors such as size, condition, recent sales, location, amenities and so forth.

It is a professional's supported opinion of the likely sales price the property would bring if offered in an open and competitive real estate market. The appraisal protects the lender from lending too much money on an asset that is not worth the loan amount. It also protects the buyer from paying too much for a property when the value is not there.

The appraisal is ordered through an independent appraisal management company (AMC). This is done so there is no affiliation and no conflict of interest between any parties involved in the transaction.

A licensed appraiser is sent to the property to measure rooms and take photos of the interior and exterior. The appraiser will also research to find three homes within close proximity and similar in style and structure that have recently sold and three similar properties that are currently on the market or in escrow.

A report is generated taking into consideration the physical inspection and the comparative market data. The value of the property listed in that report is what the lender is going to rely on to make the loan.

If the appraisal comes in low, the agents will have to get to work. If the agents agree the value is there, they may be able to submit additional comps supporting their positions based upon sales data.

If a home has updates and improvements beyond what is typical for the area, those updates may not be enough to bring up a value. More value is given on square footage and market data than the price paid for Italian marble in the master bathroom. The buyer and seller will most likely have to renegotiate the price or cancel the transaction if the agents cannot come up with supporting market data. At this point, a seller may be more likely to renegotiate as he may have a valid concern that an appraisal from a new buyer may come in at the same value or lower.

Time is of the essence in getting the appraisal ordered and back to the lender. As previously mentioned, the buyer and seller have mutually agreed in the offer to abide by timelines.

The buyer has a limited period to inspect all aspects of the property. It is very important to ensure the property is valued at or above the purchase price in order to continue with the transaction. In the event the appraisal has not been returned and the inspection time period is up, the buyer may lose a deposit in the event the appraisal comes in low and he no longer want to purchase the property.

So, after your offer is accepted,

1- Be prepared for large amount of paperwork from agents, lender and escrow

2- Order a home inspection to ensure the condition of the property is what you were anticipating. Request repair of safety items

3- Double check the paperwork from lender to make sure rate, terms, and costs have not changed

4- Wait for the appraisal to come in

# Chapter 11: Closing

When the end of the escrow period draws near, you will meet you agent at the property for your final walkthrough and verification of property condition.

The property may either be vacant now or filled with moving boxes containing the seller's belongings. If repairs were to have been made, bring the list of repairs with you so you can check specific items to see that they were completed. If there were no repairs, check to make sure everything is as you remember. If there are still large bulky items like broken swing sets or mattresses, ask your agent to make sure those items will be removed prior to you getting the keys. You should be delivered a home in at least broom clean condition without anything left to haul away.

Three days prior to the close of escrow, you should receive from your lender a Closing Disclosure. This disclosure should be very similar to the Loan Estimate you received in the beginning of the transaction. Review the document to make sure it has the loan amount, prepayment terms and interest rate you were expecting. If there are unexpected changes, call your loan officer immediately to discuss and correct if necessary.

Depending upon your state, your loan documents will be delivered to the title company, escrow, or an attorney. In California, they are delivered to escrow. You will be signing your documents in front of a notary so make sure you have with you your identification (driver's license). The notary is experienced in loan documents and may be able to assist you with general terminology. Again, make sure the documents you are signing have the same numbers (rate, term, loan amount, and fees) that you were expecting.

If the numbers are different, do not sign. At this point, you can call your agent and your loan officer and the documents may have to be redrawn. This does not happen often, but it is always important to review anything you are asked to sign. You do not want to mistakenly sign something and end up being responsible for a larger payment or different down payment that what you anticipated.

After the loan documents are signed, it's time now to send in the remaining portion of down payment. That amount is the difference between the purchase price and the loan amount (less your good faith deposit and plus any closing costs fees). You can send the money to the title company via wire or sometimes you may deliver a cashier's check. The wire is the quickest and the preferred means since there is no waiting period once the wire arrives.

So long as there are no outstanding conditions on the loan (miscellaneous paperwork from any party, final verifications of employment, etc.) the loan will be funded and the paperwork sent to the county to record the transaction. Once the transaction is recorded with the county, the transaction is complete, and you are a homeowner.

When you are ready to close, double check to make sure:

1- Repairs to the property have been made
2- The Closing Disclosure contains the numbers you were expecting
3- Your loan documents match the term, rates, amount you were expecting

# Reference Section

## Helpful Websites

The items listed in this section are for reference only. No company or entity has paid to be included in this section and no company or entity is endorsed by the Author or Publisher.

National Association of Realtors- **Confirm an agent is a Realtor®**

http://www.realtor.org/rofindrealtor.nsf/pages/fs_frealtor?opendocument
*(In addition, check state Department of Real Estate or Bureau of Real Estate site to ensure there are no complaints against the licensee or to ensure the license is active)*

Real Estate Buyers Agent Council- **ABR® Buyer's Rep Search**
http://rebac.net/buyers-rep

## Credit Bureau Websites and Addresses

Experian
P.O. Box 4500
Allen, TX 75013
http://www.experian.com/

Equifax
P.O. Box 740241
Atlanta, GA 30374

http://www.equifax.com

TransUnion
P.O. Box 6790
Fullerton, CA 92834
http://www.transunion.com

Annual Credit Request form
https://www.annualcreditreport.com/manualRequestForm.action

## Crime Information

http://crimemapping.com
http://crimereports.com
http://familywatchdog.us

## School Information
http://greatschools.org
http://globalreportcard.org

## Loan Information
USDA Loan Eligibility
http://eligibility.sc.egov.usda.gov/eligibility/welcomeAction.do
HUD               http://hud.gov
Veterans Affairs http://va.gov
VA Loan Eligibility
http://www.benefits.va.gov/homeloans/purchaseco_eligibility.asp
FHA Loan Limits https://entp.hud.gov/idapp/html/hicostlook.cfm
ARM Indexes    http://www.armindexes.com/index-types.html
Interest Rates    http://www.marketwatch.com/tools/pftools/
Loan Estimate Form
http://www.dbo.ca.gov/forms/CFPB/CFPB%20Loan%20Estimate.pdf

## Down Payment Assistance Programs

Home Buyer Rebate Programs- State Rules
http://www.justice.gov/atr/rebates-make-buying-home-less-expensive
Consumer Advocates in American Real Estate (CAARE)
http://www.caare.org/CaliforniaHomeBuyerRebates

## Home Inspectors

National Association of Home Inspectors    http://www.nahi.org/
American Society of Home Inspectors
http://www.homeinspector.org/

## Home Warranty Companies
American Home Shield                https://www.ahs.com/
Fidelity Home Warranty            https://www.homewarranty.com/
Old Republic Home Protection    https://www.orhp.com/
First American Home Warranty
https://homewarranty.firstam.com/

## Sample Dispute letter

Sample Dispute Letter to Credit Bureau (from FTC Consumer website at
http://www.consumer.ftc.gov)
[Your Name]
[Your Address]
[Your City, State, Zip Code]
[Date]

[Company Name]
[Street Address]
[City, State, Zip Code]

Dear Sir or Madam:

I am writing to dispute the following information in my file. I have circled
the items I dispute on the attached copy of the report I received.

This item [identify item(s) disputed by name of source, such as creditors or
tax court, and identify type of item, such as credit account, judgment, etc.]
is [inaccurate or incomplete] because[describe what is inaccurate or
incomplete and why]. I am requesting that the item be removed [or request
another specific change] to correct the information.

Enclosed are copies of [use this sentence if applicable and describe any
enclosed documentation, such as payment records and court documents]
supporting my position. Please reinvestigate this [these] matter[s] and
[delete or correct] the disputed item[s] as soon as possible.

Sincerely,
Your name
Enclosures: [List what you are enclosing.]

# Sample Dispute Letter 2

## Sample Dispute Letter to Creditor

Date
Your Name
Your Address
Creditor Name
Creditor Address

To Whom it May Concern,

This letter is a formal request that your company remove inaccurate credit information concerning me that you have reported to the credit bureaus.

Because of the mistake appears on my credit report, I have been wrongfully denied credit recently for a *(insert credit type for which you were denied here)*, which was highly embarrassing and has negatively impacted my lifestyle.

*(optional)* With the proof I'm attaching to this letter, I'm sure you'll agree it needs to be removed as soon as possible.

CREDITOR AGENCY - Account #123-34567-ABC

Please delete as quickly as possible.

Sincerely,

*Your Signature*
Your Name
SSN# 123-45-6789
*Attachment included*

# Afterword

Buying a house is an exciting adventure and a huge undertaking. By taking the steps I have outlined, you will reduce some of the stress involved and increase your potential for savings. By reviewing and addressing your credit prior to beginning your journey, you will ensure that you qualify for the best rates and terms available to you. You will not feel the need to accept the financing that one person offers you. Armed with your credit information and a basic understanding of loan programs, you can confidently shop for a lender or loan officer for the absolute best deal.

You now know the potential pitfalls of dual agency and how relying on the Seller's agent can cost you thousands of dollars if you're not careful. You know by looking for experience when hiring a Realtor® you can avoid costly rookie mistakes of part-timers and save money with a top negotiator. Your agent will ensure you are not taken advantage of by purchasing a home overpriced by a seller. Finally, you now know where to double and triple check paperwork and when to stop a transaction or even stop signing when things don't look right.

The goal of this book has been to help you have a greater knowledge of the home buying process and to guide you to potentially save yourself from some of the stress caused by unfamiliarity with the procedures. In the process, you may save thousands of dollars by being prepared and knowing what to ask and where to look.

Now that we have reached the end, I would like to ask a tremendous favor of you. Would you please leave feedback on Amazon regarding what you have just read? This helps me to ensure I have provided you the information that I intended, and it will help others as they search for assistance in understanding the ins and outs of buying a home.

Also, if you have any additional questions, please feel free to contact me. I am currently an active and licensed Realtor® and Broker in the

State of California. If you are in my state, feel free to contact me for any assistance or representation you may need. If you are located outside of California, I may not be familiar with your state laws, but I am always willing to assist and provide guidance if I can. Feel free to contact me if you run into an issue or if you have any questions with which I may be able to provide answers. My email address is DawnAndersonMarketing@gmail.com

# One Last Thing...

Now that you have read this book will you please visit Amazon.com and provide some feedback for me? If you believe the book is worth sharing, please would you take a few seconds to let your friends know about it? If it turns out to make a difference in their lives, they'll be forever grateful to you, as will I.

All the best,


Dawn.

www.ingramcontent.com/pod-product-compliance
Lightning Source LLC
Chambersburg PA
CBHW060641210326
41520CB00010B/1697